Contents

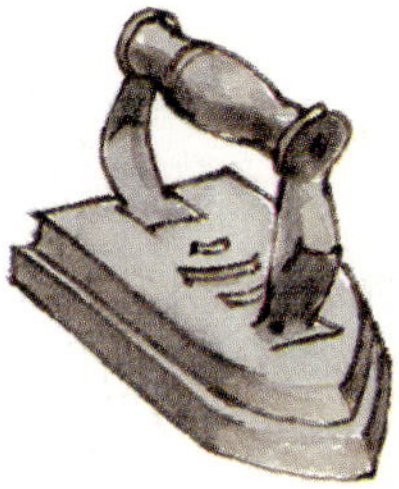

1 Meet Richard

Detective work

Look carefully at the photograph and the pictures.

1 What does Richard look like? Write a brief description of him.

2 What are his hobbies?

3 When is his birthday?

4 Where does he live?

5 a How old was he in 1986 when this book was written?
  b Which clues helped you to work this out?

Hello there! Meet Richard. This book is all about Richard and his family. But it's not just a story-book. It's all true.

As you read it, you will be doing some detective work. You will be looking at clues and using them to find out about Richard and his grandma.

You can see some clues about Richard on these pages. There is a photograph of him and some pictures of his favourite things.

Richard's favourite things

2 Richard's family album

A

Richard has a sister called Helen. Richard and Helen love to look at photographs of when they were little. They also like to see photographs of their Grandma's childhood.

One day Richard decided to make a family album. He asked Grandma to help. On these pages you can see four of the photographs they put in their album. They show Richard, Helen and Grandma when they were little children.

B

Look carefully at the photographs.

1 a Which photographs show Richard and Helen and which show Grandma?

b What clues in the photographs helped you to tell the difference?

2 a Is Helen older or younger than Richard?

b How can you tell?

3 The photographs are jumbled up. Can you put them in the right order? Start with the photograph taken first.

C

D

3 Looking back in time

Grandma as a little girl, 1918

"How long is it since you were a girl, Grandma?" asked Richard one day.

"Too long!" laughed Grandma. "Look, I'll draw you a time line and then you can work it out for yourself."

Below you can see Grandma's time line.

It shows when Grandma, her brother, Richard and Helen were born. The pictures show how Grandma has changed over the years.

In 1918 Grandma was two years old. This was the last year of World War One

In 1938 Grandma got married. In 1939 World War Two started

Detective work

1 Look back along the time line and find the year Grandma was born.

2 How many years is it since Grandma was ten years old?

3 What important event was happening when Grandma was born?

4 Look at the photo of Grandma's father. Why is he wearing a uniform?

5 How has Grandma's life changed over the years?

Richard in 1986

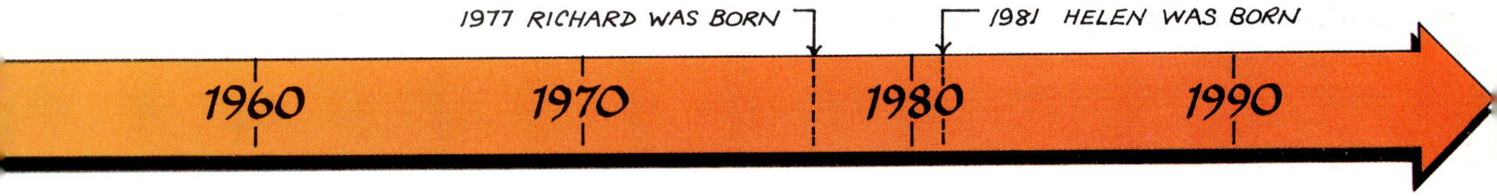

By 1958 Grandma had children of her own

By 1978 Grandma had her first grandson, Richard

4 Grandma's family

A

Grandma's family. Grandma aged 6 (her name was Nellie), little brother Albert, aged 2, her father George Horbury and her mother, Lily Horbury.

Richard's Grandma often told him her memories of her childhood.

"Were things different then?" asked Richard.

"Yes," said Grandma. "Lots of things have changed since I was a girl. Now where are those old photographs? You'll find some clues in them."

Look at the pictures on these pages.

Picture A is a photograph of Grandma as a girl with her parents and baby brother.

Picture B is a drawing of Richard's grandad as a little boy and his family.

Detective work

1 How many differences can you spot between your family today and Richard's grandparents' families sixty years ago?

2 How were baby boys dressed sixty years ago? Try to find out why.

3 Richard's grandad didn't have a photograph of all his family together. What do you think is the reason for this?

4 In what way would a real photo of Richard's grandad's family have been different from this drawing?

Richard's grandad's family

B

5 Grandma's home

One day Grandma showed Richard the house where she grew up. Richard asked what it had been like inside.

"Our house had two rooms upstairs, two rooms downstairs and a **cellar**," she began. "We only used the front room on special days like Christmas. Most of the time we lived in the kitchen. There wasn't much space to play.

I shared a bed with my little brother. We were lucky. Many families – like Grandad's – had six or eight children. They had to sleep four to a bed – two at the top and two at the bottom."

Grandma's home (in the middle of the picture)

Detective work

1. Read Grandma's description of the house where she grew up. Make a list of any differences you notice between Grandma's life in her house and your life in your house today.
2. Look at the drawing of Grandma's kitchen. How many differences can you spot between this and your kitchen at home?
3. Grandma's family didn't use their front room very much. What do you think was the reason for this?

Grandma's kitchen

6 Wash-day and bath-night

A little girl in a tin bath

"How did you keep clean?" asked Richard. "You didn't have a bathroom!" So Grandma told him her memories of wash-day and bath-night.

"We used to get bathed in the kitchen on a Friday night," she explained. "Our mother had to light a fire under the **copper boiler** to heat some water. Then she had to pour the hot water into a tin bath by the fire. The rest of the week we kept the tin bath down in the cellar.

It took all day Monday to do the washing. First mother put the clothes in a dolly tub of hot, soapy water. Then she jiggled them up and down with the peggy legs. After that she scrubbed them on the rubbing board. She had to heat the irons in the fire before she could do the ironing."

Detective work

1 Look back at the picture of Grandma's kitchen on page 11. Try to find the copper boiler where the water was heated.

2 Why were the clothes washed by hand?

3 Look at the pictures opposite. How did Grandma's mother squeeze the water out of the wet clothes?

4 Why did she have to heat the irons in the fire?

5 Why do you think she needed two irons?

6 Was it harder or easier to keep clean sixty years ago than it is today? Give reasons for your answer.

Grandma's mother (on the right) hanging out her washing

Peggy legs, dolly tub and rubbing board

A mangle for squeezing the water out of wet clothes

Two flat irons

7 Whistling in the dark

Are you afraid of the dark? Sometimes Richard is. But sometimes he thinks it's exciting – like on Hallowe'en night. Once Grandma described how she felt about the dark as a child.

"When I was a girl there were more dark places than today," she told him. "We had only candles and a **paraffin lamp** in those days.

Three dark places used to frighten me. At bedtime I didn't like going up the stairs. They were narrow and steep. Our candle used to flicker and make strange shadows on the walls.

I didn't like going down to the cellar either, to get coal for the fire. We kept food down there too, on a big stone table. Even on a sunny day the cellar was cold and dim. It always had a funny, musty smell.

Then there was the **midden**. This was a little stone building across the back yard where the toilets were. These weren't proper flush toilets like we have now – they were just earth closets. At night I used to run across the back yard very fast. I always kept the toilet door half-open. Then I used to whistle. Somehow, whistling made me feel less afraid."

Going upstairs to bed

Down in the cellar

Running across the back yard to the midden

Detective work

1 Why were there more dark places when Grandma was a girl than there are today?

2 Why do you think people kept food down in the cellar?

3 Grandma told Richard that she didn't have a "proper flush toilet – just an earth closet". Try to find out what she meant.

4 How do you feel about the dark? Write a story and draw a picture about the dark.

8 The back yard

"If there was no room to play in your house, where did you play?" asked Richard. "And what toys did you have?"

"We liked spring and summer best," explained Grandma. "Then we could play out in the back yard. One day someone would shout 'The oranges have come in at Parker's shop!'. Then we would all dash down to ask for the ropes from the orange boxes. These were our skipping ropes. In those days you couldn't buy oranges all year round like today.

The boys used to ask the butcher for **animal bladders**. They made these into footballs. Most toys were home-made. You were very lucky if you had a toy from a shop. I remember I had a pram and a doll made from goatskin."

Detective work

Look at the picture of children playing in a back yard sixty years ago.

1 Make a list of the games Grandma and her friends used to play.

2 How many of Grandma's games do you still play today?

3 Which of your games did Grandma and her friends not play? Try to explain why.

4 Why do you think most toys were home-made?

5 Why do you think Grandma's doll was made from goatskin?

9 Neighbours

Grandma showed Richard the back yard where she had played. Some of the houses had been knocked down. But the middens were still there, and the **blacksmith's** workshop. This workshop was now a garage.

"Who else lived here?" asked Richard.

Grandma made him a list of all the neighbours she knew as a child.

Neighbours	Their jobs	Their children
Tom and Lucy Middleton	QUARRYMAN	Harry, Jim and Edith
"Granny" Cowling	MIDWIFE	Bill, Matt and Ernie
Jim and Lucy Hebden	CARRIER	Muriel, Ted and Irene
Mr and Mrs Saynor	Schoolteacher	Peter
Sam and Mary Burton	COAL-MINER	Violet, Bob, Ivy, Sid, Ted, Jim, Leslie and twins who died
George and Lily Horbury	Coal-miner	Nellie and Albert
Joe and Martha Chambers	Quarryman	Lottie, Blanche, Myra, Vincent, Elsie and Frank
Tom and Emma Rhodes	Quarryman	Nellie and Alice
Ernest and Fanny Chapman	Quarryman	Connie, Elsie, Clifford, Etta, Ernie, Dorothy, Ivy, Ted, Ken, and twins who died
George and Mary Terry	Coal-miner	June
Jim and Ada Scott	Coal-miner	Florence and Joe
Benny and Emily Greaves	Blacksmith	One child who died

Detective work

1 Work out how many children there were in each family. Then make a bar chart.

2 How many families had children who died? Try to find out why children died in the 1920s. Your grandparents may be able to help.

3 Look at the pictures of "Granny" Cowling, Jim Hebden and Benny Greaves. How would each of their jobs be different today?

"Granny Cowling used to deliver babies. As soon as a baby started coming the family sent for her. She'd put on a clean pinny and off she'd go. I don't think she had any training. Most babies were born at home."

"Jim Hebden had a lorry. Every Friday night he rigged up a canvas roof and put seats in the back. Then on Saturday, he took people off to town."

"Benny Greaves did a lot of work for the farmers in the village. He put shoes on their horses, mended their carts and steam engines. He made all kinds of iron tools."

10 A day's work

"What about going to work? Was that different too?" Richard wanted to know. So Grandma told him her memories of her father's work.

"My father was a coal-miner like many men in our lane," she began. "When he was on early **shift**, my mother had to get up at 4 o'clock in the morning. She had to light a fire before she could boil a kettle. Some people paid a knocker-up. He came round the street, tapping on the bedroom windows with a long stick.

Knocking up the miners for work

The miners set off for work about 5 o'clock. They had to walk the three miles [five kilometres] to the **pit**. They all carried their **snap tins** with their bread and dripping and bottle of cold tea. I can still hear the noise of their wooden clogs going down the street. If men were late, they were sent home. Then they used to take their clogs off and walk up the lane in their bare feet.

A miner at the coal face

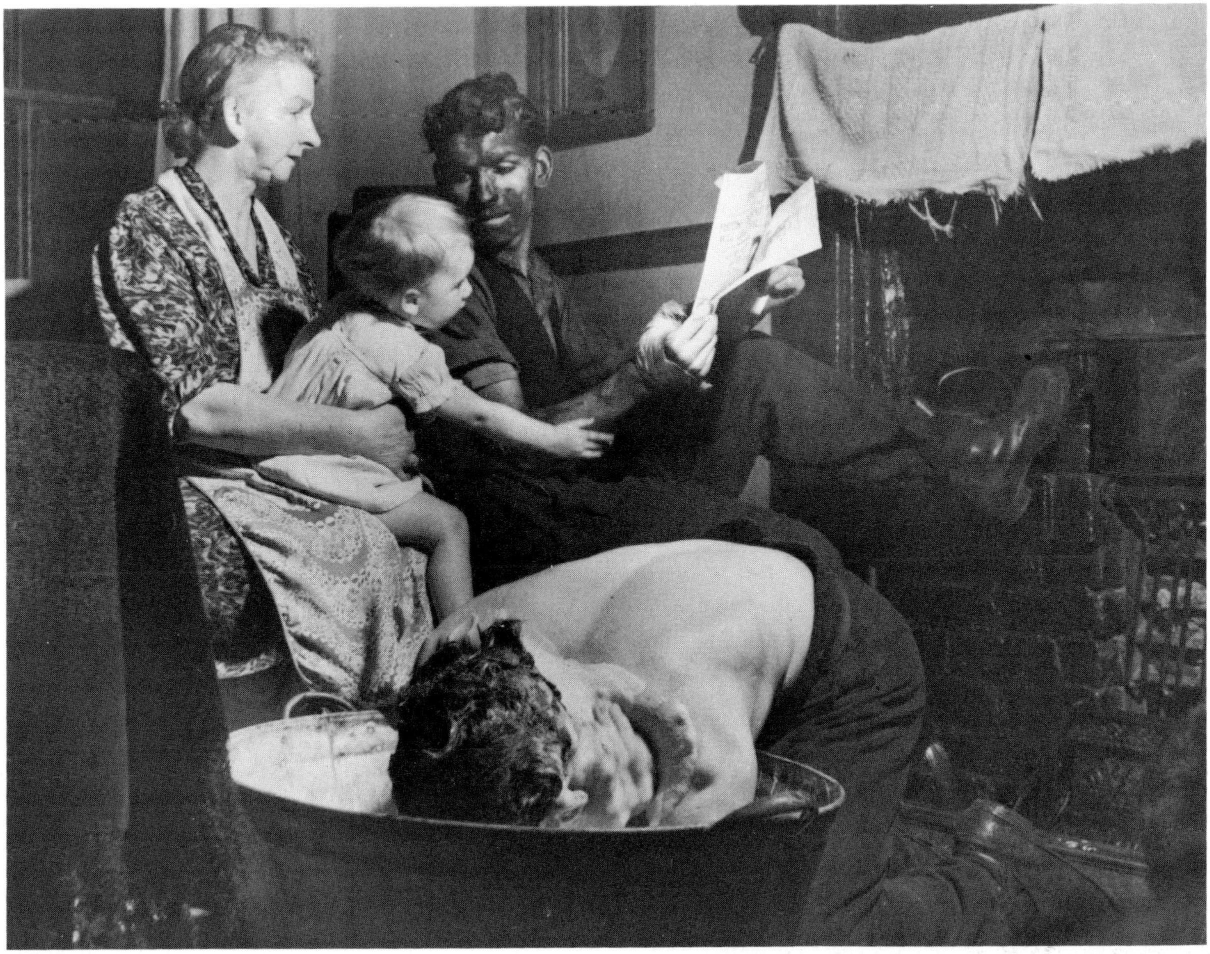

This miner is washing away the coal dust

When my father came home he was covered in coal dust. He used to keep his dirty pit clothes in a box. Sometimes we could hear something squeaking. Then we knew a mouse had got into his pocket down the pit."

Detective work

1 Why do you think people needed a knocker-up sixty years ago?

2 Why do you think miners walked up the lane in bare feet if they were sent home?

3 In what ways is the life of a coal-miner different today?

4 In what ways is the life of a coal-miner's wife different today?

11 Hard times

Grandma told Richard a lot about her everyday life. But he wanted to know about her feelings too.

"Were you happy as a girl, Grandma?" he asked.

"Yes, we had many happy times," she said, "but there were hard times too.

I remember the miners' strike of 1926. The mine-owners wanted the men to work longer hours for less pay. The miners said no and stopped work. The strike went on for over six months. That meant six months with no wages coming in.

The children used to go off 'sticking' – collecting sticks for the fire. We had no coal. We went round the fields looking for turnip tops. The farmers used to cut these off before they fed the turnips to the sheep. We took them home for a stew.

Someone set up a big cooking pot outside the old soldiers' club. Miners' children could go and get free soup. My brother and I went a few times but then we stopped. I felt too ashamed sitting by the road with my bowl."

Queuing for free soup

Queuing for bread during the strike

Detective work

1 In 1926 Grandma's father earned about 9 shillings a day (45p). But the pits did not work every day. If he worked three days a week, how much could he earn?

2 The mine-owners wanted him to work for 7 shillings a day (35p). If he worked three days a week for this pay, how much would he earn?

3 Look at the list of some of the things Grandma's family spent money on each week.

	"Old" money	"New" money
Rent	4s 6d	23p
Groceries	15s 0d	75p
Meat	5s 6d	28p
Milk	1s 2d	6p
Paraffin	6d	3p
Total	26s 8d	135p

4 Why didn't the miners want to work for 7 shillings a day?

12 A day at the seaside

Richard always looks forward to his summer holiday at the seaside. But he hates the long journey in the car. One day Richard came across an old photograph of the seaside sixty years ago. He asked Grandma if she could remember a holiday by the sea.

"When I was a girl, I never had a real holiday," she told him. "A few times I went on a day trip to the seaside with the Sunday School.

The night before, I couldn't sleep for excitement. We had to get up at the crack of dawn and walk two miles [three kilometres] to the station. I thought the train was marvellous. I can still remember the hissing of the engine and the smell of the steam.

I couldn't wait for my first glimpse of the sparkling sea. We loved playing on the sands with our buckets and spades."

Grandma and her brother loved steam trains

Read Grandma's memories and look at the pictures.

1 Grandma said that ordinary families didn't go away on holiday when she was a girl. Talk to your grandparents and try to find out why.

2 In what ways was Grandma's journey to the seaside different from Richard's?

3 Make a list of ways in which Grandma's day on the beach as a girl would have differed from Richard's seaside holiday today.

13 Shopping

Every Thursday night Richard and his Dad go shopping at the supermarket. Richard wheels the trolley round. Then he helps to load the boxes into the car. Grandma's memories of shopping are different.

"When I was a girl you didn't see men shopping – or pushing prams!" she laughed. "I used to take our order to the Co-op grocery shop on a Monday. This was for things like tea, flour, sugar, lard, soap, potatoes, candles and matches. We didn't buy

The Co-op grocery shop

bread. In those days most people baked their own. On Thursday the Co-op delivery man brought the orders round with a horse and cart.

The butcher's shop was just at the bottom of the lane. We used to go down and buy meat each day. A man came round with a cart selling vegetables and apples twice a week. But lots of people had **allotments** and grew their own vegetables."

Detective work

Look at the picture and read Grandma's memories.

1 How many differences can you spot between a supermarket and Grandma's grocery shop?

2 Why do you think Grandma went to buy meat each day?

3 Grandma said men didn't do the shopping when she was a girl. What do you think were the reasons for this?

4 Find out the cost of your family's weekly shopping bill today. Compare it with Grandma's bill. What differences can you see?

Grandma's weekly shopping bill, 1926		
Butcher's bill	5s 6d	(28p)
Grocery bill	15s 0d	(75p)
Milk	1s 2d	(6p)
Paraffin	6d	(3p)

Some prices, 1926		
Joint of meat	1s 11d	(10p)
12lb potatoes	1s 0d	(5p)
24 oranges	1s 0d	(5p)
1 pint milk	2d	(less than 1p)
pint of paraffin	2d	(less than 1p)

14 Looking for clues

Richard enjoyed finding out about Grandma's life as a little girl. "It's a bit like doing detective work," he said.

"I suppose so," replied Grandma, "except you are trying to discover what happened in time past instead of today."

Detective work

1 Look at the picture of Richard and Grandma below and the pictures on the opposite page. What clues helped Richard to find out about Grandma's childhood? The clue boxes at the bottom of the page will help you check your answer.

Clue 1

m _ _ _ r _ _ s

Clue 2

_ h _ _ _ _ r _ p _ _

1 Everyday objects

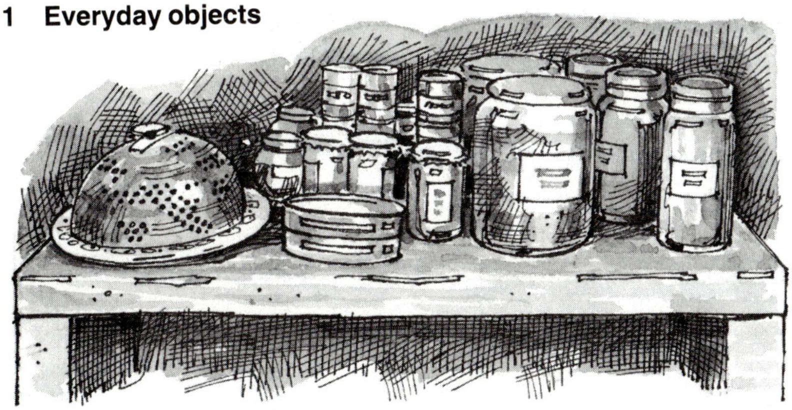

"We didn't have a fridge. We kept food on a stone slab down in the cellar."

- Why was the cellar a good place to keep food?

Grandma's memories and photos helped Richard to discover different things about ...

2 Her thoughts and feelings

- How do you think Grandma was feeling here?

3 Differences between the 1920s and today

- In what ways was Grandma's doll different from dolls today?

15 Then and now

Grandma told Richard that many things were different when she was a girl. Life for ordinary families has changed between then and now. The pictures on these pages show some of the changes.

Detective work

Quiz

1 Look at the *Objects* in pictures A, B and C.
   a What did Grandma use these objects for?
   b What objects do we use today instead?

2 Look at the *Going places* pictures, D, E and F.
   a In what ways would these journeys be different today?
   b In what ways would these places have changed since Grandma was a girl?

3 Look at the *Problems* pictures, G, H and I . What changes or inventions have helped to solve these problems?

4 Look at all the pictures again. Name anything in these pictures which might still be the same today.

Objects

A

B

C

Going places

Problems

16 What words mean

allotment a small piece of land that you pay to use as a garden; people grow vegetables and flowers on their allotments

animal bladder a small skin bag inside an animal which stores waste water

blacksmith a man who makes horseshoes, tools and other things out of iron

carrier a man who makes a living carrying goods on a lorry

cellar a room underneath a house or building, used for storing things like coal

coal-miner a man who works down a mine getting coal

copper boiler a kind of brick stove for heating water; it had a metal pot set in a square of bricks with a space for a fire below; when the fire was lit, it heated the water

midden an outside building where the toilets were

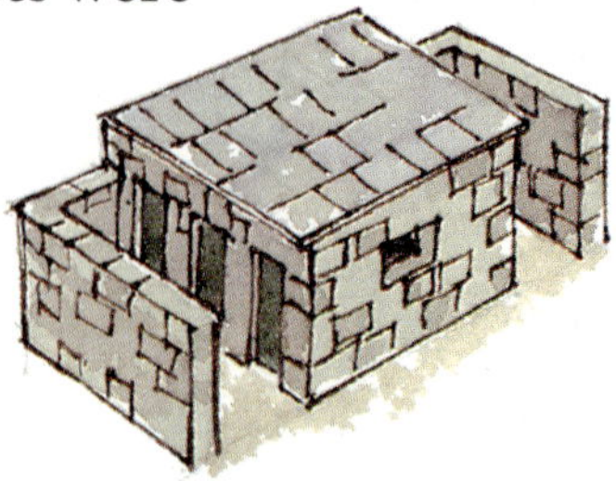

midwife someone who delivers babies

paraffin lamp a lamp which made light by burning paraffin (a kind of oil)

pit a coal mine

quarryman a man who works in a quarry (a big hole in the ground where men dig for stone)

shift an eight-hour work period for miners down the pit: there were usually three shifts in a day
Early shift: some miners worked 6am to 2pm
Afternoon shift: some miners worked 2pm to 10pm
Night shift: some miners worked 10pm to 2am

snap tin a miner's lunch-box